JUMP INTO JOBS

WEATHER JOBS

Written by Kay Barnham
Illustrations by Jennifer Naalchi

Enslow PUBLISHING

Published in 2026 by Enslow Publishing, LLC
2544 Clinton Street
Buffalo, NY 14224

First published in Great Britain in 2022
by Wayland

Editor: Amy Pimperton
Designer: Lisa Peacock

Cataloging-in-Publication Data

Names: Barnham, Kay. | Naalchigar, Jennifer, illustrator.
Title: Weather jobs / Kay Barnham, illustrations by Jennifer Naalchigar.
Description: Buffalo, NY : Enslow Publishing, 2026. | Series: Jump into jobs | Includes glossary and index.
Identifiers: ISBN 9781978545779 (pbk.) | ISBN 9781978545786 (library bound) | ISBN 9781978545793 (ebook)
Subjects: LCSH: Meteorology--Vocational guidance--Juvenile literature. | Climatology--Vocational guidance--Juvenile literature. | Weather--Juvenile literature.
Classification: LCC QC869.5 B376 2026 | DDC 551.5023--dc23

Manufactured in the United States of America

CPSIA compliance information: Batch #CSENS26:
For further information contact Enslow Publishing LLC, New York, New York at 1-800-398-2504.

Please visit our website, www.enslowpublishing.com.
For a free color catalog of all our high-quality books, call toll free 1-800-398-2504 or fax 1-877-980-4454.

Find us on

CONTENTS

MEET BILLIE ... AND MIA!

Here are some of the things that Billie likes best: Mia the cat, science, storms, and asking lots of questions like these ...

(Here are some of the things that Mia likes best: eating, snoozing in the sunshine, umbrellas, Billie.)

One day, Billie would love to work with weather. But which is the best job to do? There are so many to choose from!

Luckily, Billie's dress-up box can help. When Billie and Mia pick something to wear, magic happens. Instantly, they whoosh away to meet people who do all sorts of awesome jobs.

This time, Billie picks sunglasses and an umbrella. These are perfect for a weather adventure filled with sunshine and showers.

METEOROLOGISTS … ARE WEATHER EXPERTS

METEOROLOGISTS are scientists who study the weather to find out how it works. They predict the weather too.

Meteorology is the science that studies the atmosphere. This is the blanket of air around our planet and it's where weather happens.

Weather satellites orbiting Earth collect data from the atmosphere. This data is used to create satellite images.

This satellite picture shows where in the world it is raining and where it might rain next!

Meanwhile, weather stations all around the world take measurements, such as temperature, wind speed, and rainfall.

Meteorologists spot weather patterns in the data. They use these patterns to predict what the weather will be tomorrow, next week, or even further into the future.

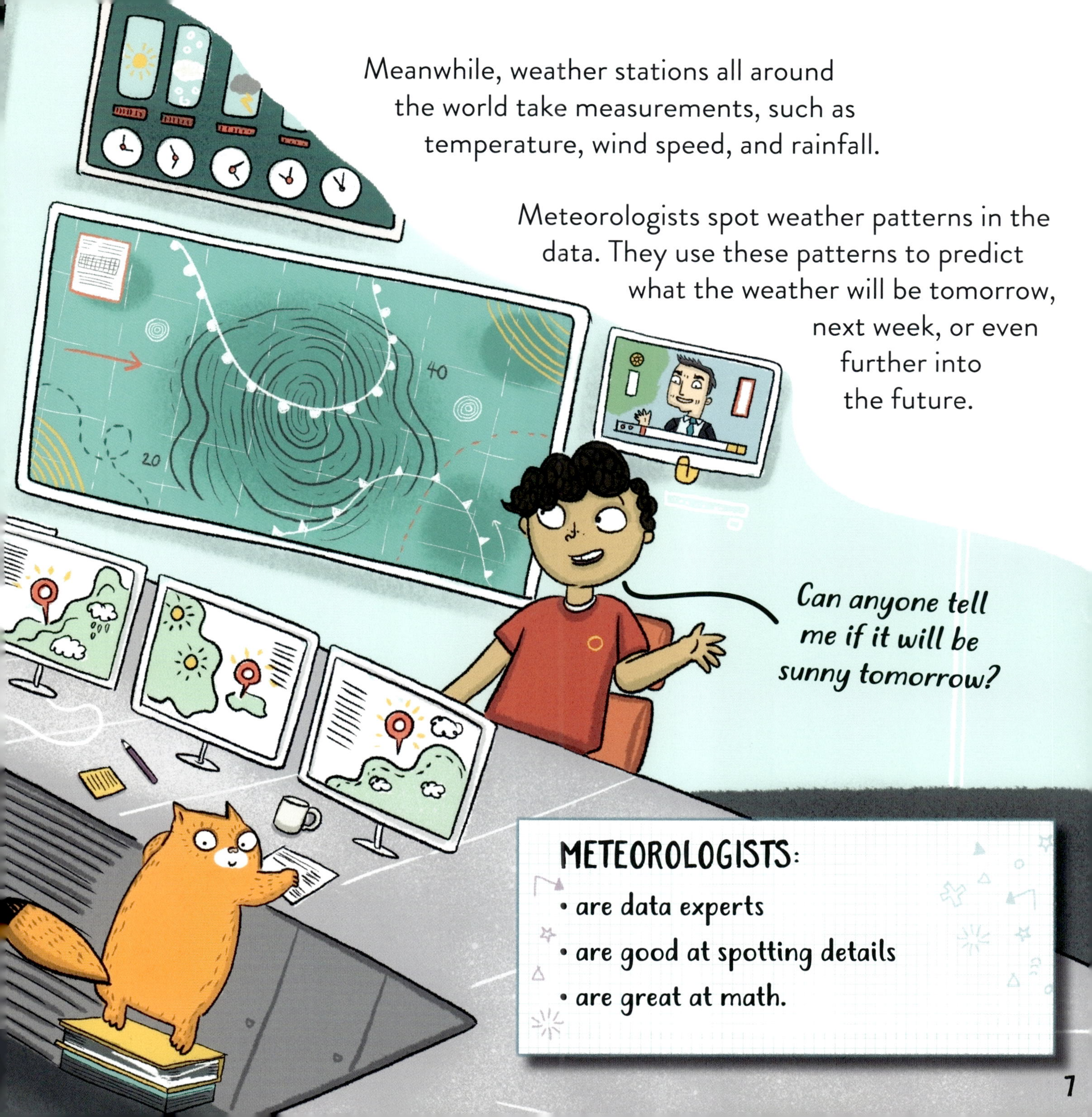

METEOROLOGISTS:

- are data experts
- are good at spotting details
- are great at math.

WEATHER PRESENTERS ...
TELL US ABOUT WEATHER

If you're not a meteorologist, weather data can be very confusing. **WEATHER PRESENTERS** explain the weather forecast in a clear way, so everyone can understand.

It's a weather presenter's job to tell the story of the local or national weather over the next few days. Their forecasts can help you to decide whether to wear rain boots, go sledding, fly a kite, or head to the beach!

When bad weather is due, weather presenters give people as much warning as possible. If a hurricane is coming, it's a good idea to know about it!

WEATHER PRESENTERS:

- understand geography • are confident speakers
- can tell a weather story in an interesting way.

AVALANCHE FORECASTERS ...

... KEEP PEOPLE SAFE

When snow, ice, and rock tumble down a mountainside, it's called an avalanche. Because avalanches can be deadly, **AVALANCHE FORECASTERS** are on the alert for them.

An avalanche happens when more snow falls on a snowy mountain. If an older layer of snow gives way under the weight of the new snow, the top layer can slide off and cause a dangerous avalanche.

Avalanche forecasters try to work out where avalanches are going to happen. They also keep a close eye on the weather, because heavy snowfall means a bigger chance of an avalanche. Sometimes, they start avalanches on purpose to make the slopes safer for people.

AVALANCHE FORECASTERS:

• know about different types of snow • are expert skiers

• can handle dangerous explosives.

STORM CHASERS ... INVESTIGATE STORMS

Menacing storm clouds, crazy lightning, and deadly tornadoes are spectacular types of weather. **STORM CHASERS** will drive a long way to investigate them.

Tornadoes are spinning columns of air that form beneath storm clouds and spiral down to the ground. The very biggest tornadoes can cause a lot of damage.

Tornadoes are hard to predict. But experienced storm chasers are skilled at guessing where a tornado might appear.

Storm chasers use probes to gather scientific data – such as wind speed and temperature – from inside a tornado. They might film what actually happens in there too. This helps to reveal the science of how tornadoes work.

STORM CHASERS:

- are quick thinkers • love collecting data
- don't mind driving long distances.

HURRICANE HUNTERS ... FLY THROUGH STORMS

Tropical cyclones – or hurricanes – are giant storms that form over warm oceans. The brave pilots that zoom into these storms are called **HURRICANE HUNTERS**.

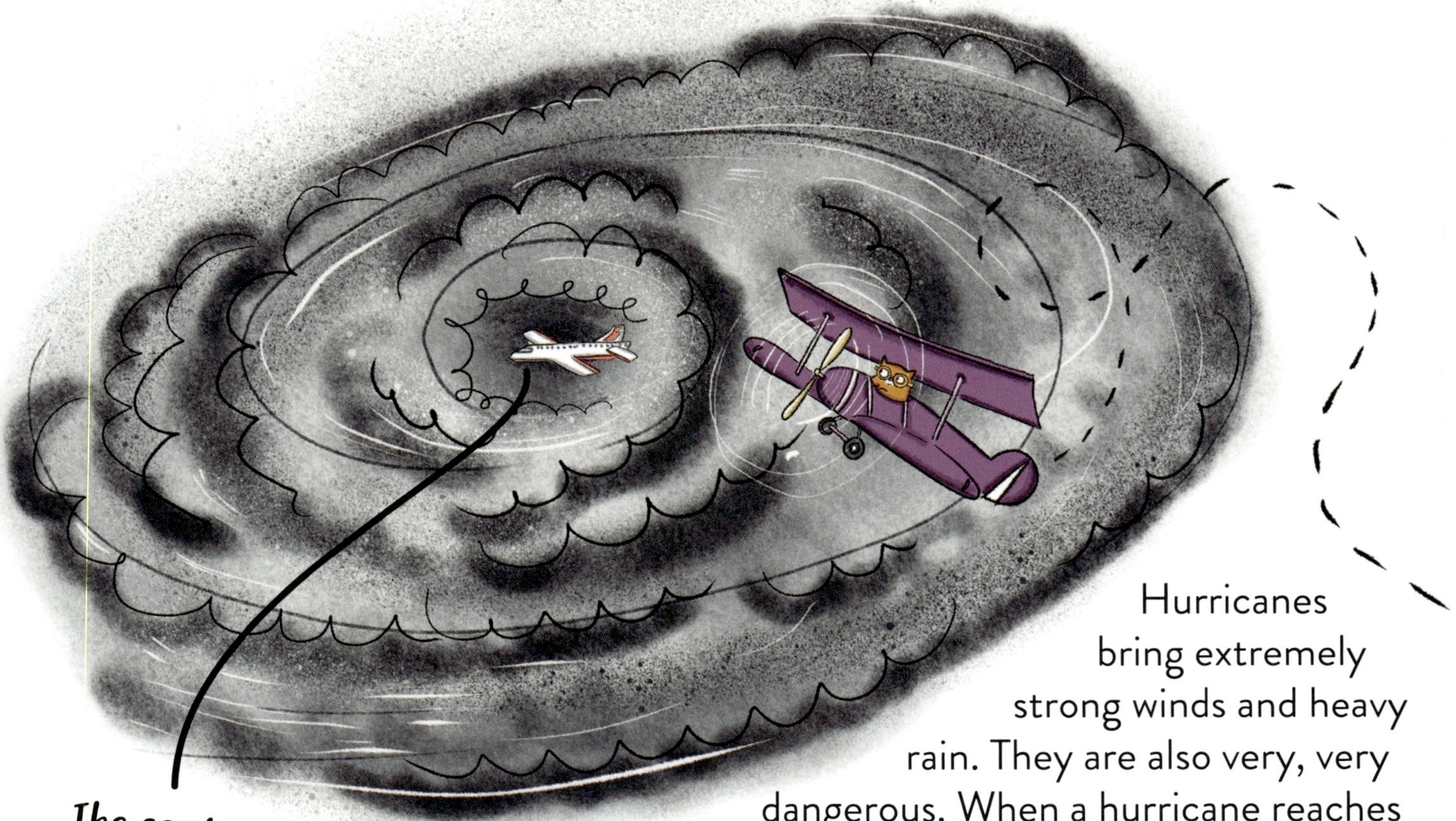

The center of a hurricane is called "the eye of the storm."

Hurricanes bring extremely strong winds and heavy rain. They are also very, very dangerous. When a hurricane reaches a coastline and then travels over land, it can cause a lot of damage.

Hurricane hunters fly right into a storm ... and out the other side! They use weather instruments to take measurements from the hurricane, such as wind direction, speed, and temperature. This information is used by meteorologists to work out where the hurricane is heading. If people can get out of its way, lives may be saved!

HURRICANE HUNTERS:

• are expert pilots • are very brave • stay calm under pressure.

SOLAR FARMERS ... HARVEST THE SUN'S ENERGY

SOLAR FARMERS fill their fields with lots of solar panels. These are used to turn the sun's energy into electricity.

Sometimes, solar farmers grow crops too. The land beneath the solar panels is the perfect place to grow vegetables that need some shade. Wildflowers grow here too, creating a new habitat for bees and other wildlife!

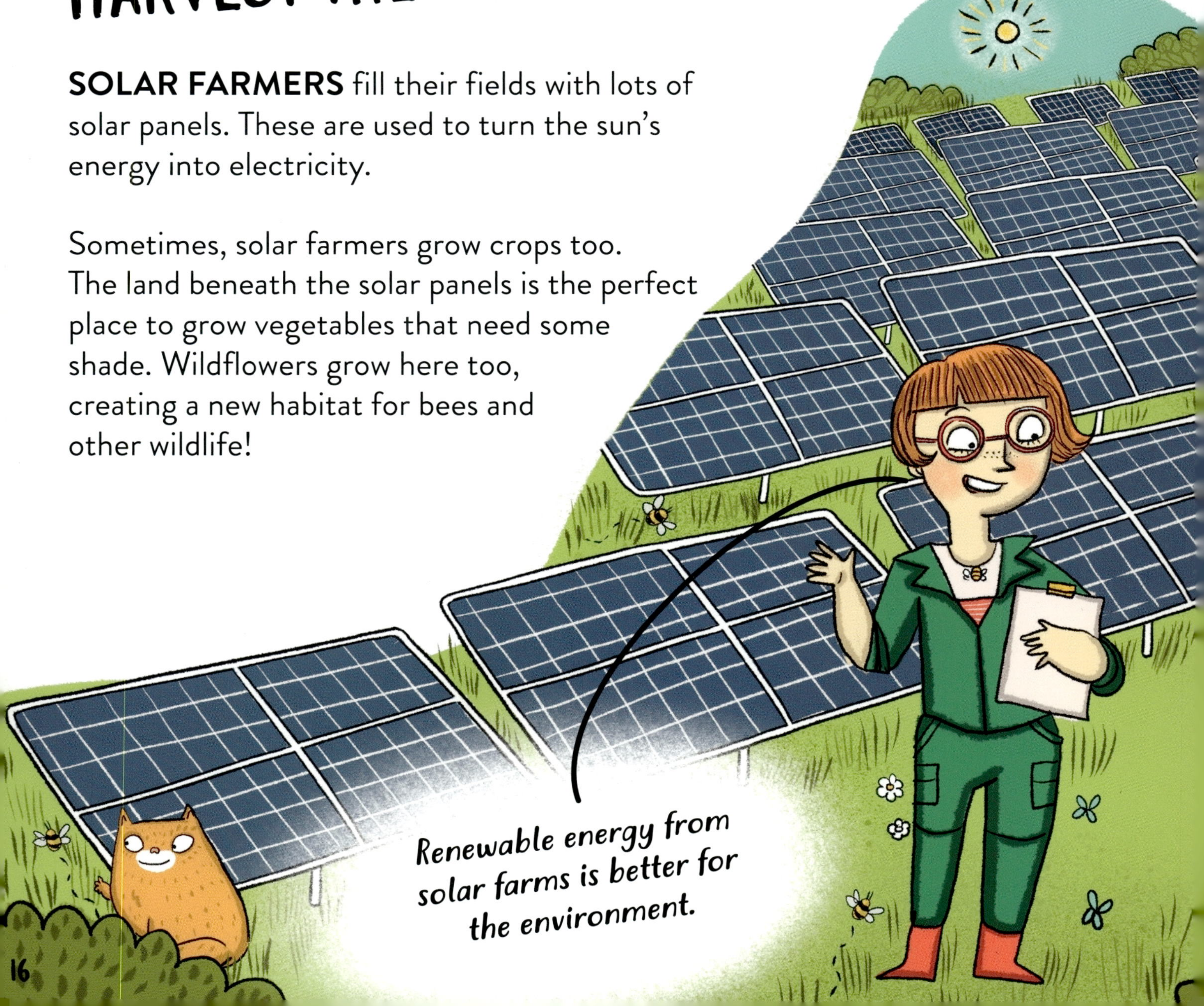

Fossil fuels – such as coal – can be used only once. Renewable energy sources – such as sunlight, wind, or waves – can be used over and over again.

On a solar farm, there might be thousands of solar panels! It's a solar farmer's job to make sure these are working properly.

SOLAR FARMERS:

- are electrical engineers
- love working outdoors
- are eager to help the environment.

CLIMATOLOGISTS ... FORECAST FUTURE WEATHER

CLIMATOLOGISTS don't just look at the weather today. They study years' of weather reports. This helps them to predict what the weather will be like in the future.

A climate is a pattern of weather – these are different all over the world. Places near the equator usually have a hot and wet tropical climate. Places near the north and south poles have a polar climate – here, the weather is very, very cold!

By recording the weather for a long time, climatologists can see if climates are changing. Climatologists also study how human activity – such as burning fossil fuels and cutting down rainforests – causes global warming.

Climatologists predict what could happen to our planet if temperatures continue to rise.

CLIMATOLOGISTS:

- are interested in finding out more about climate change
- carry out research • like to study the past.

HYDROLOGISTS... STUDY THE WATER CYCLE

HYDROLOGISTS study water as it moves around our planet. For example, some hydrologists are experts in why some rivers flood.

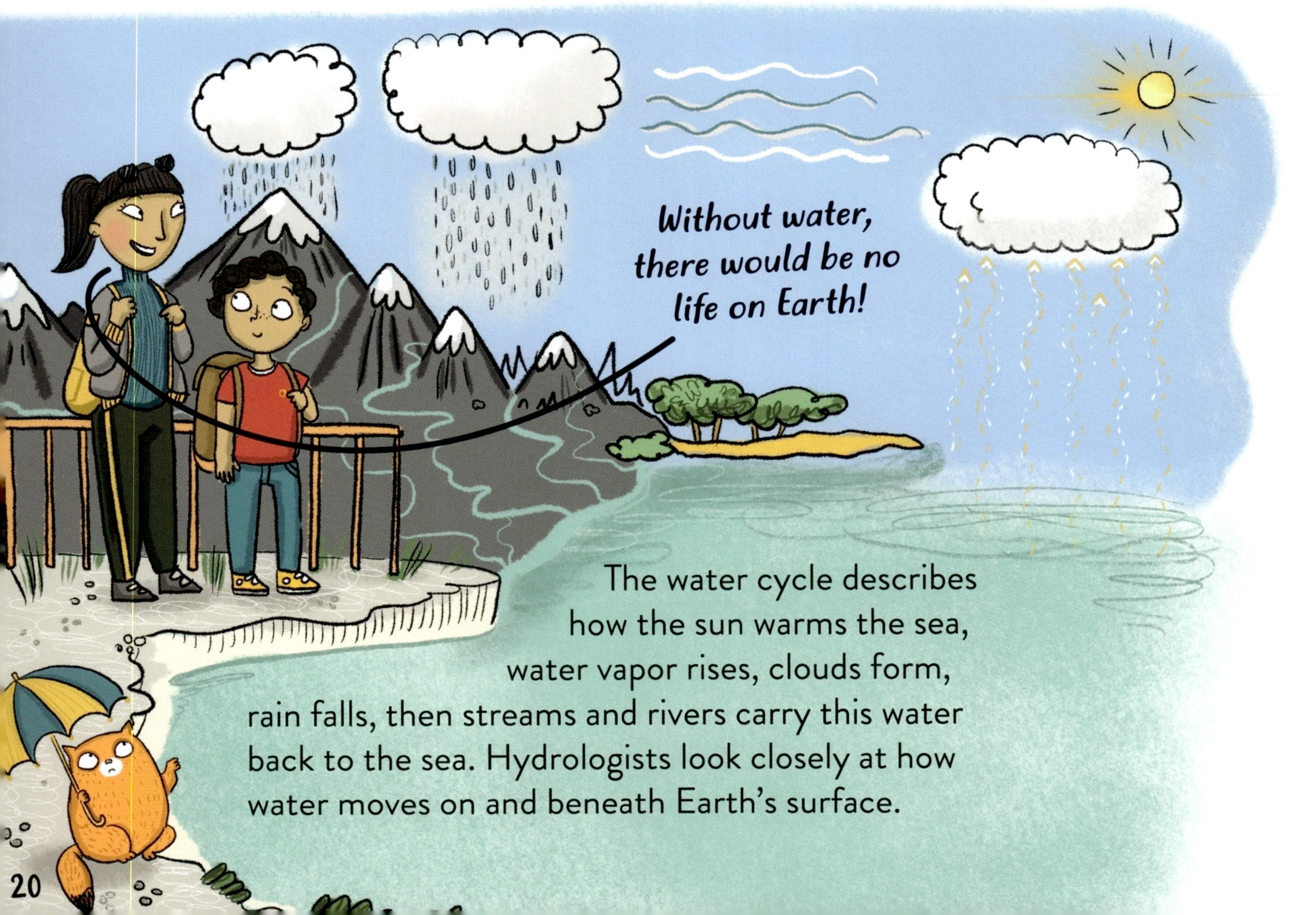

The water cycle describes how the sun warms the sea, water vapor rises, clouds form, rain falls, then streams and rivers carry this water back to the sea. Hydrologists look closely at how water moves on and beneath Earth's surface.

Studying pollution is a very important part of a hydrologist's job. By taking samples of water and soil, they find out if a water supply is polluted. Then they suggest ways to fix the problem.

HYDROLOGISTS:

- investigate the environment
- are passionate about water
- are great at problem-solving.

LIGHTNING STEEPLEJACKS ... PROTECT BUILDINGS

When a skyscraper is struck by lightning, why doesn't it burst into flames? The answer is ... the building has been lightning-proofed by a **LIGHTNING STEEPLEJACK**!

Lightning steeplejacks climb tall structures to attach a special metal lightning rod to the highest point. The rod is attached to a strip of metal that runs down the outside of the building to the ground.

A lightning bolt contains about a billion volts of electricity – which can be very dangerous. It can start fires, damage equipment, or harm anyone who gets in the way. But when lightning strikes a lightning rod, electricity travels safely to the ground down the metal strip.

LIGHTNING STEEPLEJACKS:

- are super fit
- aren't afraid of heights
- understand how electricity works.

WEATHER PHOTOGRAPHERS ...
TAKE STUNNING SHOTS

A flash of lightning, a swirling tornado, or a beautiful rainbow happen very quickly. By capturing these images, a **WEATHER PHOTOGRAPHER** can make them last for ever.

Photographers' images appear in newspapers, magazines, books, and online. They are used by companies who want to advertise their products. Some photographs are works of art, hanging in galleries or homes.

Weather photographers need to be prepared. They check the weather forecast to find out if it will be stormy, sunny, or misty.

They also need to be ready for anything. If a ray of sunlight shines between rain clouds, it's time to take a photo of that beautiful rainbow ... NOW!

WEATHER PHOTOGRAPHERS:

- are artistic
- are very patient
- have great technical skills.

SPACE WEATHER FORECASTERS ... STUDY THE SUN

The sun is a superhot sphere of gases that glow brightly. **SPACE WEATHER FORECASTERS** track the sun's activity and predict how this will affect Earth and spacecraft.

The sun's surface is very active. Solar flares are explosions and sunspots are cooler areas that appear and vanish. Meanwhile, solar winds speed toward our planet. This space weather can damage spacecraft and cause losses of power on Earth.

Space weather forecasters use special equipment to collect huge amounts of sun data. Forecasters can then predict space weather for hours or even weeks into the future. This helps scientists to know when to move spacecraft if a solar flare is on the way.

SPACE WEATHER FORECASTERS:

- are meteorologists
- are space scientists
- have superb computer skills.

NOW IT'S YOUR TURN TO WORK WITH WEATHER!

Like Billie and Mia, are you inspired by the weather? Set up your own weather station and record weather as it happens!

1. Make your own weather book. Include as much information as you can find for each day. For example:

- record the date
- record what type of weather it is each day
- record if it is cold, warm, or hot. You can use a thermometer or find the temperature on a TV weather forecast or in a weather app.

2. Make a rain gauge to measure how much rain falls. Ask an adult to cut the bottom off a plastic bottle and leave it in the open. Remember to mark measurements on the side of the bottle.

3. Make an anemometer to measure wind speed. Attach four paper cups to straws and attach these to the top of a pencil. Hold it in the air and make a note of how fast it spins.

Ask an adult to help you with these activities and when using scissors or glue.

GLOSSARY

advertise to tell people about a product, often with pictures

confident when a person is sure of themselves and how well they can do something

cyclone a giant storm that forms over warm oceans; another word for hurricane

environment the natural world

explosives chemicals used to blow things up

forecaster someone who tries to work out what will happen in the future

fossil fuels types of fuel made from the remains of plants and animals over millions of years, such as coal and gas

habitat the natural home of an animal, plant, or other living thing

hurricane a giant storm that forms over warm oceans; another word for cyclone

instrument a tool used to measure things; a tool that does a precise job

measurement how big or small something is

meteorologist a scientist who studies the weather

renewable something that can be used again and again

satellite a spacecraft that orbits (travels around) a planet

solar panel a flat, rectangular device that collects energy from the sun's rays

volt a measurement of electricity

weather station a place where weather conditions and data are recorded

FURTHER INFORMATION

BOOKS TO READ

Banks, Rosie. *Meteorologist*. New York, NY: Scientific American Educational Publishing, an imprint of Rosen Publishing, 2025.

Morlock, Rachael. *Storm Chaser*. Buffalo, NY: PowerKids Press, 2026.

Wargula, Doris. *Air Masses and Weather Fronts*. Buffalo, NY: Britannica Educational Publishing, 2025.

WEBSITES TO VISIT

Learn more about weather and prediction at the National Oceanic and Atmospheric Administration (NOAA) website for kids.
https://scijinks.gov/

Find out more about space weather on this NASA website.
spaceplace.nasa.gov/spaceweather/en/

INDEX